The CPR Retirement Rescue Roadmap

YOUR GUIDE TO BREATHING LIFE INTO ANY PORTFOLIO

Nathaniel J. Miller

Miller Retirement Group

LAWRENCE, KANSAS

Nathaniel J. Miller/Miller Retirement Group
805 New Hampshire, Suite B
Lawrence, KS 66044
http://www.millerretirementgroup.com/

Book layout ©2013 BookDesignTemplates.com

Ordering information:
For details, contact the address above.

The CPR Retirement Rescue Roadmap/ Nathaniel J. Miller. —1st ed.
ISBN 978-1539658528

Contents

Contents

To all retirees:
May your golden years be not gold plated, but solid gold.

CHAPTER 1

My First Memory of Money

When I was 6 years old, I had my very first experience with money, and that memory has impacted every financial decision I have ever made. I remember sitting down in front of our TV and VCR, (I'm dating myself here), and telling my mother that it was OK for her to sell all of my Ninja Turtle video cassettes if it would make some money for the farm because, even though my parents thought we weren't really listening to some of their conversations, I had picked up on the fact that the farm didn't do so well that year.

I was one of six children living in that farmhouse, and there were definitely some lean years early on. That laughable Ninja Turtle offering was my little 6-year-old brain's way of helping my parents out financially. Some of you may have felt this feeling before. You know what feeling I'm talking about; that feeling in the pit of your stomach of not having enough money. I felt that feeling all the time while growing up, and even after leaving the farm, I unknowingly carried it into adulthood.

Because of that experience, I always found myself drawn to the financial services industry, whether it was taxes or banking, but it wasn't until I found this retirement planning niche of the financial services industry that I found a way to truly help people with their finances, like my little 6-year-old-self wanted to so long ago.

I happened upon the industry by chance, and it's one of those things that, when you look back on it, you know it happened for a reason. I started working for a firm that consulted for insurance agents and financial advisors, collectively referred to as financial professionals, all across the country. This firm had minimum premium requirements that a financial professional had to produce before it would consider working with them. That minimum premium requirement eliminated a huge majority, considering the income of the company's financial professionals was 2 ½ times the 2014 median average income of a financial advisor, $81,060.[1] So, if we were to apply the 80/20 rule, the company only wanted to work with that 20 percent of financial professionals who were responsible for 80 percent of a typical business.

I was blessed to have worked with about 125 of those elite financial professionals; financial professionals who have been on TV, have their own radio shows, have been quoted in or published numerous articles in The Wall Street Journal, The New York Times and more. This was the best education I could get in retirement planning! I looked at it as access to learn the strategies and techniques from some of the top minds in retirement planning.

I absorbed everything I could and attended as many training events as I had time for, driven by the unconscious need to keep that feeling in my stomach from ever coming back. I quickly learned these financial professionals were very specific about who they worked with. They focused on people who were either already in retirement or were very close to retirement, and I quickly

---

[1] U.S. News. "Best Jobs: Financial Advisor Overview." http://money.usnews.com/careers/best-jobs/financial-advisor. Accessed Aug. 30, 2016.

realized they truly cared for the people they worked with. I had found an industry with heart.

After about a year of being exposed to this, I got my own licenses and began splitting time between consulting with financial professionals and running my own practice. I became a marketing resource, banking up knowledge about income planning product selection. Soon I had financial professionals looking to me for product expertise and assistance in identifying the best products for their clients, but I found myself becoming more and more fulfilled when working in my own practice. Finally, I made the decision to stop splitting my time and focus solely on building my own retirement planning practice.

Now I make a commitment to you. When I do my job correctly, my ultimate objective is to make certain you never have that feeling in your gut in retirement. I am blessed to now get to make a living by helping clients work toward financial independence so they don't have to experience the feeling in retirement that affected me so much in my early life. This is not just a job to me. It's personal. It's emotional. I treat every retirement plan I design as if it were my own money. Since I know what that horrible feeling is like, I will do everything in my power to keep you from experiencing it. That is why I wrote this book. This book tells the story of everything I take into account during my planning process and just like the title suggests, can provide you with a road map to help keep you on the path to a more confident retirement! It's time for you to enjoy the retirement you've earned!

CHAPTER 2

Budgeting Is a 4-Letter Word

The last time I ever overdrew my checking account was in my early 20s. I remember it because I had overdrawn pretty badly. I remember sitting down in a Wendy's with an older gentleman, a mentor of sorts, whom I went to for financial advice quite often.

This time, I was up the creek without the proverbial paddle. I didn't know how I was going to make rent. I was afraid they were going to come and take my car, and my next paycheck would barely be enough to even cover the overdraft fees. I even remember crying on the phone to a bank representative to see if they would be willing to waive the overdraft charges. And now, as I recounted all of this to him, here I was, a grown man, choking back tears in front of my mentor. I explained that I didn't know how this kept happening. I wasn't going out and getting drunk. I rarely ate out, and if I did it was the McDonald's dollar menu. How could this keep happening?

Now, he had recommended that I create a budget and write down all my expenses for a full month multiple times in the past. So instead of getting down in the pit of despair with me, he simply asked, (even though he knew the answer), "Have you written down your expenses for a full month? Are you using cash for the fluctuating expense categories?" I think you know what my answer was. Remember at the beginning of this chapter I mentioned that this was the last time I ever overdrew my checking account? I implemented his advice after that. Funny how sometimes it takes banging your head against the same wall multiple times before your ears pop out far enough to listen!

Maybe I should apologize for even uttering the word "budgeting," only because so many people hate doing it. I take that back, I'm actually not sorry. One of the most basic things that can derail a retirement is not knowing what you spend. In my opinion, it's also the easiest thing to fix. When I sit down with people and I ask them what their monthly net income is and what their monthly expenses are, they usually know what their paycheck says, so they are pretty darn accurate when it comes to their income, but the expenses are another story. Usually they start looking at each other, saying "Let's see, our mortgage is $1200 a month, our car payment is $300 a month, what do we pay in utilities, hon? Oh, and the cable bill is..." You get the idea. They are trying to make it up on the spot because they have no budget. When I say they have no budget, what I mean is they have nothing written down that tells where each dollar should go every single month. Usually I will hear something about how their net income is $5,000 a month and their expenses are $3,000 a month, but I have a litmus test for a real budget.

I will say, "OK, it looks like you have an extra $2,000 every month. How much of that are you saving over and above what you are contributing to your 401(k) or retirement plan at work? Because that comes out of your paycheck and has already been factored into the net number you told me earlier. So how much of that $2,000 per month are you saving?"

"Oh. We're not saving any of it."

To which my response is, "OK, then it looks like your expenses are more like $5000 per month, would that be accurate?"

"Yep, I guess they're $5000 per month."

Can you imagine being $2000 a month off on what you think your spending is? You had better imagine it, because it happens all the time. A written budget can fix that.

Now, if you are one of the sick few who, like myself, love spreadsheets and happen to have your budget sitting on a spreadsheet on your computer with automatic formulas that compute your savings, your tithes, mortgage, utilities, etc., then you can probably skip the rest of this chapter. If you are "normal," however, you should probably keep reading.

The first thing I am going to recommend is what I did after that meeting in Wendy's in my early 20s. I wouldn't recommend anything to you that I am not willing to do, or have not done. Write down every single expense for one month. Keep a journal of every single expenditure that you spend your money on for one whole month. This includes the Dr Pepper and candy bar you bought at the convenience store when you filled up for gas. Your mortgage or rent and utilities. It includes the pack of gum you bought. Everything.

Then put all of that into categories. Categories can be food, mortgage, insurance, entertainment, clothing, blow money. If you've never worked off of a budget before, start by using cash for the categories like entertainment, clothing and blow money; categories that for some are easily overspent. For example, you're not going to overspend on your mortgage. It's pretty much the same every month, hopefully. Your car insurance is the same every month, but your entertainment can fluctuate, so putting a limit — in cash — on what you can spend will keep you from just swiping your debit card or credit card and buying something you probably shouldn't.

For those who feel working off of a budget sounds restrictive, take it from me and the many people I've coached who have done this successfully: You actually feel a sense of freedom when you truly get it down. You experience freedom because now you tell every dollar where it goes instead of the other way around. You can now make life happen instead of letting life happen to you.

In my opinion, getting a handle on your budget before you enter retirement is critically important to keeping you on the path to your financial goals.

CHAPTER 3

Debt: Most People You Think Are Well Off May Just Be Broke at a Higher Level

I married my lovely, infinitely patient wife, whose taste in men is apparently tall, bald and gangly, on April 26, 2008. Earlier that year I decided to lead a Dave Ramsey course at our church. Not because I thought I knew everything about how to manage finances yet, but because I still had a good amount of credit card debt and student loan debt that I wanted to get rid of.

When you grow up a certain way, you perpetuate those habits until you learn new ones. Part of my earlier money issues were carryovers from that mentality, and, having been exposed to new ways of thinking, I was starving for more information on how to better my financial position. I decided to lead the Dave Ramsey course because I believed it would also help me eliminate my debt faster. Instead of merely going through the course as a participant, I thought if I led the course, it would keep me that much more accountable to doing what was recommended, and in order to be a good example to the rest of the class, I would be forced to succeed.

It worked.

I stroked the last check for the last bit of non-mortgage debt about a year later.

I am going to give you a very simple formula to help you eliminate debt. It is the one that I followed. You can do this with what you currently make. And, if you have created a budget like I mentioned in the previous chapter, you should be able to find the discretionary income I will talk about.

Step 1: On the left-hand side of a sheet of paper, write down every debt you have, other than your mortgage. This includes every car payment you have, every credit card, every department store card, every student loan, everything.

Step 2: To the right of every debt, write down the remaining balance of each debt.

Step 3: Grab another sheet of paper and write down each debt, from smallest remaining balance at the top to the largest remaining balance at the bottom.

Step 4: To the right of each balance, write down the minimum monthly payment of each debt.

Step 5: Below all of the debts, write down the amount of discretionary income you have left after all of your expenses. This is the amount that you will apply to the first debt that has the smallest balance, the debt listed at the top of this page.

Step 6: You will pay the minimum amount on every other debt. Once you have paid off the debt with the smallest balance, you will move that entire amount, the minimum payment plus your discretionary amount, to the next largest remaining balance.

Step 7: Once you pay off that debt, then you will move the entire amount to the next largest debt. The following illustration should give you an idea of what this will look like as you move the amounts from one debt to the next. In this example, we have assumed that $200 is the discretionary amount that you have left to put toward debt.

Creditor	Total Debt	Regular Payment	Regular + Extra Payment	New Payment
Target account	$450	$25	$25 + $200	$225
Shell account	$600	$40	$40 + $225	$265
Master Card account	$850	$75	$75 + $265	$340
Parent loan	$1,200	$150	$150 + $340	$490
Car loan	$8,000	$350	$350 + $490	$840

Repeat until debt-free!

CHAPTER 4

Employer-Sponsored Retirement Plans: A Ticking Tax Time Bomb?

4 01(k), 403(b), 457 plan, IRA... all are different names for different employer-sponsored retirement plans. Which one do you have, and what does it mean?

All of these names are probably a little confusing. I like to simplify things. This is going to be a generalization, but most people are familiar with the 401(k). 401(k) is generally for employees of privately owned companies. 403(b) is generally for teachers or other public employees. Basically, the biggest difference for what it is called is based off of where you work. However, the 401(k), and all of the above, except the Roth IRA, (we'll cover that later), from a tax standpoint are all generally treated the same: You contribute to each one on a pretax basis, meaning you get a deduction for it in the year you contribute and, therefore, pay no taxes on it, nor do you pay taxes on the growth of those assets. Instead, when you retire and pull the money out, that is when you are taxed on it. This is what we call a tax-deferred retirement account. Tax deferred means that you pay no tax on the contribution and no tax on the growth of the account until you make a withdrawal. This not only allows the principal to grow without being taxed, but also the interest on the principal can grow without being taxed.

That all sounds great while you are working! However, when you retire, these accounts often amount to being your highest tax liability, because this is money you have never paid taxes on. The idea was that you would set money aside while you worked, and you wouldn't pay any taxes on that money. You had the expectation that it would grow, tax deferred, over time, and at some point in the future you would begin taking money out for retirement. But often people forget that you do, at some point, pay taxes on it, and so these accounts slowly became a bigger and bigger tax liability!

Now we need to talk about an exit strategy. An exit strategy is a way of leaving a current situation after you have met a specific objective. Specifically, a graceful tax exit strategy is a means of reducing taxes on the income you plan to receive during retirement. And if you do nothing, the government happens to have an exit strategy for you. What happens if you are 70 ½ years old and have qualified money? What do you have to do? Mandatory withdrawals. They are called required minimum distributions, or RMDs for short. The government says you have to take that money out. If you do not, you can be penalized up to a 50 percent tax penalty on the amount you should have taken out. That's a hefty penalty. For some, required minimum distributions may not be the best strategy.

Here is an example of a 65-year-old couple who has $500,000 in their retirement plans. We're going to assume conservative 5 percent average earnings. Let's also say they live to age 90. You may say, "Live to age 90?" The reality is that one of you is likely to live to age 90. Most of the time, it will be the wife. If you look at the illustration, what are the total required distributions over their lifetime?

	Age		Beginning	5.00%	RMD	RMD	Ending
Required Minimum Distribution Spreadsheet $500,000 5% Earnings Hypothetical Example	Beg Year	End Year	Value	Earnings	Divisor*	Withdrawn	Value
	65	66	$500,000	$25,000		$0	$525,000
	66	67	$525,000	$26,250		$0	$551,250
	67	68	$551,250	$27,563		$0	$578,813
	68	69	$578,813	$28,941		$0	$607,753
	69	70	$607,753	$30,388		$0	$638,141
	70	71	$638,141	$31,907	26.5	$24,081	$645,967
Divisor based on information from The IRS Minimum Distribution Worksheet*	71	72	$645,967	$32,298	25.6	$25,233	$653,032
	72	73	$653,032	$32,652	24.7	$26,439	$659,245
	73	74	$659,245	$32,962	23.8	$27,699	$664,508
	74	75	$664,508	$33,225	22.9	$29,018	$668,716
	75	76	$668,716	$33,436	22.0	$30,396	$671,755
	76	77	$671,755	$33,588	21.2	$31,687	$673,657
	77	78	$673,657	$33,683	20.3	$33,185	$674,154
	78	79	$674,154	$33,708	19.5	$34,572	$673,290
	79	80	$673,290	$33,665	18.7	$36,005	$670,950
This hypothetical example is for illustrative purposes only, and should no be deemed a representation of past or future results, and is no guarantee of return or future performance. This example does not represent any specific product and/or service. The information is believed to be reliable but the accuracy of the information cannot be guaranteed. Be sure to speak with qualified professionals before making any decision about your personal situatoin.	80	81	$670,950	$33,547	17.9	$37,483	$667,014
	81	82	$667,014	$33,351	17.1	$39,007	$661,358
	82	83	$661,358	$33,068	16.3	$40,574	$653,852
	83	84	$653,852	$32,693	15.5	$42,184	$644,360
	84	85	$644,360	$32,218	14.8	$43,538	$633,041
	85	86	$633,041	$31,652	14.1	$44,896	$619,796
	86	87	$619,796	$30,990	13.4	$46,253	$604,533
	87	88	$604,533	$30,227	12.7	$47,601	$587,158
	88	89	$587,158	$29,358	12.0	$48,930	$567,586
	89	90	$567,586	$28,370	11.4	$49,788	$546,177
				Taxable Dist.		$738,569	
					Total Taxable Dist.		$1,284,746
					30% Tax		$385,424

They are required to withdraw and pay tax on how much money? $738,569. So they are going to pay tax on over $700,000 of distributions on an IRA that was how big to start? $500,000. But are we done paying taxes? No, because once they die, their kids still have that $546,177 left in the account. Is that tax free? No, that is going to get taxed, too. So if mom and dad paid taxes on $738,569 of distributions, the kids still have $546,177 to pay taxes on, so that is $1.28 million that the family will collectively pay taxes on. If we pay a 30 percent tax rate, that is almost $400,000 in taxes.

That is a lot of taxes. Very close to the amount that we started out with! However, with a prepared exit strategy, we can potentially reduce those taxes.

If you look at the following illustration of "The Four Tax Buckets," you will see the continuum of how your money is taxed.

To help reduce taxes in the future, you should consider taking action today. In fact, the more money you have, the more advantageous it can be to move assets to the right on the tax bucket continuum. But, because the goal is to reduce the total amount of taxes you pay in retirement, you may have to take on a greater tax bill today. You can do this by strategically repositioning assets from Bucket 1 and Bucket 2, to Buckets 3 and 4 to reduce retirement income taxes as much as possible. You should work with a financial advisor who works very closely with a qualified tax professional regarding your individual situation to find out what may make the most sense for you.

CHAPTER 5

Real Historical Returns of the Stock Market

S it down with a big-name wirehouse financial advisor, and at some point during the conversation they will likely tell you that the stock market "long-term" average is a 10 percent rate of return. They love to point to the last 70 years in an attempt to prove the case. If you asked them to define "long-term," they will almost certainly say, "10 years or longer." And they are not wrong. Over the last 70 years the market *has* averaged a 10 percent return per year. But here's my question: We have market data going all the way back to 1896, *so why are we using just part of the data and not all of it?*

Once we start looking at all the data, the answer becomes very clear. All of the data does not support a 10 percent average return.

I like to use numbers, not just words, so I looked at the entire history of the Dow Jones since it started, or at least since we have data on it, in 1896. You can get the data yourself from www.djindexes.com.

Then, after taking the year-by-year returns, I grouped them into decades. I started with 1900 - 1909, then 1910 - 1919, and so on. I started with 1900 instead of 1896, because I didn't want to make it complicated with off-year decades, so the analysis does leave out a few years, but it still makes the point. Check out the following illustration to learn how the market performed in each decade.

Decade	Return
1900-1909	+4.19%
1910-1919	+0.80%
1920-1929	+8.77%
1930-1939	+4.92%
1940-1949	+2.95%
1950-1959	+12.98%
1960-1969	+1.65%
1970-1979	+0.47%
1980-1989	+12.62%
1990-1999	+15.37%
2000-2009	.0007%
Average Return	**+4.98%**

Now, it is important to note that dividends are not included in these numbers. Dividends vary throughout the years, so feel free to plug in your own. The first thing you notice is that, out of the 11 decades represented, only three of them broke the classic 10 percent per year return. But what about the other eight decades? After all, aren't they the majority? If you look at those decades, you find that they will normally fall far short of the 10 percent per year average. So what does this tell us? The majority of the time, 73 percent, the market returns far less than the touted 10 percent average rate of return. Only 27 percent of the decades beat it. Let's generously call it a 70/30 split. You only have a 30 percent chance of beating a 10 percent return, and a 70 percent chance of falling far short of your target.

Do you also see patterns in the data? How about this? The market seems to have a tendency of low returns, or pretty flat returns, over a 20-year period. And then it takes off for a decade. What do I mean? Look at 1900 through 1919. You see 20 years of lower returns. Then, suddenly, the decade of the 1920s goes crazy. Next, 1930-1949. 20 more years of lower returns. Then the 1950s hit, and it's boom time. Following is 1960 to 1979, more blah years. But then the pattern broke, and we had *two* good decades in a row, the 1980s in the 1990s. This was unprecedented growth! But what happens in the 2000s? Back to more blah.

The old strategy of buy-and-hold works great when times are good, and the 1980s and 90s were great examples of that. It doesn't work so well, though, in the low-return years. During those time periods, essentially inside the dash between the two dates, your account balances look like a roller coaster. Basically, you see a bunch of ups and downs, but overall you're not really going anywhere. And during your retirement years, you can't afford to ride a roller coaster that goes nowhere.

CHAPTER 6

Sequence of Returns

A very smart, numbers savvy, young gentleman of the age of 35 realized, if he put $5,000 a year away into an investment account and it averaged 10 percent per year, by the time he was ready to retire at 65, he would have amassed close to $1 million dollars! Or, $991,964.14, to be exact.

At the end of 30 years, he averaged 9.68 percent! Really close, right? And by the way, we are taking any fees out of the equation here. So this is 9.68 percent after fees.

So what do you think his account balance would be? Pretty darn close to $1,000,000, right? Then why is it only $562,821? Almost half of what he had figured? Well, he was a victim of "sequence of returns." Before I go too in depth on this example, take a look at another illustration.

This shows the same 35-year-old putting the same $5,000 a year into an investment account, and averaging the same 9.68 percent. The end result here? $1,031,968! That's actually more than if he averaged 10 percent every year! How in the world did that happen? Take a look at the following charts to compare.

Sequence of Returns Risk: Chart 1

Age	Earnings Rate	Ending Balance	Age	Earnings Rate	Ending Balance
35	25.77%	$6,289	51	20.26%	$284,996
36	-9.73%	$10,190	52	31.01%	$379,919
37	14.76%	$17,433	53	26.67%	$487,571
38	17.27%	$26,307	54	19.53%	$588,751
39	1.40%	$31,745	55	-10.14%	$533,549
40	26.33%	$46,422	56	-13.04%	$468,308
41	14.62%	$58,940	57	-23.37%	$362,715
42	2.03%	$65,236	58	26.38%	$464,720
43	12.40%	$78,946	59	8.99%	$511,964
44	27.25%	$106,822	60	3.00%	$532,478
45	-6.56%	$104,487	61	13.62%	$610,679
46	26.31%	$138,290	62	3.53%	$637,410
47	4.46%	$149,686	63	-38.49%	$395,173
48	7.06%	$165,600	64	23.45%	$494,031
49	-1.54%	$167,974	65	12.78%	$562,821
50	34.11%	$231,976	Average	9.68%	

This hypothetical example is for illustrative purposes only, and should not be deemed a representation of past or future results, and is no guarantee of return or future performance. This example does not represent any specific product and/or service.

Sequence of Returns Risk: Chart 2

Age	Earnings Rate	Ending Balance	Age	Earnings Rate	Ending Balance
35	12.78%	$5,639	51	-1.54%	$199,024
36	23.45%	$13,134	52	7.06%	$218,428
37	-38.49%	$11,154	53	4.46%	$233,393
38	3.53%	$16,724	54	26.31%	$301,114
39	13.62%	$24,683	55	-6.56%	$286,033
40	3.00%	$30,574	56	27.25%	$370,340
41	8.99%	$38,772	57	12.40%	$421,882
42	26.38%	$55,319	58	2.03%	$435,548
43	-23.37%	$46,222	59	14.62%	$504,956
44	-13.04%	$44,543	60	26.33%	$644,227
45	-10.14%	$44,519	61	1.40%	$658,316
46	19.53%	$59,190	62	17.27%	$777,871
47	26.67%	$81,310	63	14.76%	$898,423
48	31.01%	$113,075	64	-9.73%	$815,520
49	20.26%	$141,997	65	25.77%	$1,031,968
50	34.11%	$231,976	Average	9.68%	

This hypothetical example is for illustrative purposes only, and should not be deemed a representation of past or future results, and is no guarantee of return or future performance. This example does not represent any specific product and/or service.

Well, once again it was "sequence of returns." In retirement, we don't know what sequence returns will come in, or if they will be positive or negative. That poses a potential risk. In the first illustration, you will notice that there is a pretty substantial loss close to the end: 38.49 percent. Sounds like 2008 doesn't it? The significance of this is that he had a very large loss within the "Retirement Red Zone." What the heck is the Retirement Red Zone? Well, do you know what the red zone is in football? In football, you are in the red zone when you are inside the 20-yard line, close to scoring.

In the retirement world, the red zone is the 10 years before you retire, and the 10 years after you retire; they could arguably be the most important years in your financial lives! If you aren't working with an advisor who specializes in this phase of your financial life, you need to find one immediately. If you experience large losses during this time, it can have a significant negative effect on your retirement portfolio! The reason being, you have a much larger amount in the account than early in your saving career, so a large percentage loss means a larger dollar amount loss.

In the second illustration, that 38.49 percent loss occurs in the third year of saving, when he had a very small amount accumulated. I know what you're thinking: 38.49 percent? Isn't that the same amount the first illustration lost three years from the end? Yes it is. Because here's the crazy part: these are the exact same returns, only the second illustration is the first illustration flipped upside down, so the returns are coming in reverse order.

We are led to believe the most important return to consider is your average return. However, more important than average return is the sequence of those returns. While we can see the importance of this during the Accumulation phase of our financial life, (more on that terminology later), it becomes infinitely more important during our retirement years, or the Decumulation phase, (once again, more on this later).

CHAPTER 7

Dollar-Cost Averaging
us.
Reuerse Dollar-Cost Averaging

I would like to introduce you to two brothers, Bill and Steve. Bill and Steve were very much alike. They were both financially savvy. They both had good jobs. They both even managed to save the exact same amount in their IRAs during their working years. They each saved $500,000. Not only that, but they each only needed to pull $30,000 a year out of their IRA in order to supplement their retirement income. There was only one difference in this example. Steve retired in 1990. Bill retired in 2000. What was the result?

At the end of 10 years, while still taking $30,000 out per year, Steve's portfolio is doing fantastic! He has more than he started with! He has $1.2 million and change! His portfolio at this rate should be able to last another 10 years with no problem. Bill on the other hand is not so lucky. He is left with only $152,000 and change. Why such a huge difference? They each started with the same amount, and they each took the same amount out every year.

Income and Sequence of Returns

Steve
Retired in 1990

Bill
Retired in 2000

End of Year	Market Return	Withdrawal	IRA Account Balance	End of Year	Market Return	Withdrawal	IRA Account Balance
1990	-4.34%	$30,000	$449,602	2000	-6.18%	$30,000	$44 0,954
1991	20.32%	$30,000	$504,865	2001	-7.10%	$30,000	$381,776
1992	4.17%	$30,000	$494,667	2002	-16.76%	$30,000	$292,819
1993	13.72%	$30,000	$528,419	2003	25.32%	$30,000	$329,364
1994	2.14%	$30,000	$509,085	2004	3.15%	$30,000	$308,794
1995	33.45%	$30,000	$639,340	2005	-0.61%	$30,000	$277,094
1996	26.01%	$30,000	$767,829	2006	16.29%	$30,000	$287,345
1997	22.64%	$30,000	$904,873	2007	6.43%	$30,000	$273,892
1998	16.10%	$30,000	$1,015,728	2008	-33.84%	$30,000	$161,359
1999	25.22%	$30,000	$1,234,328	2009	18.82%	$30,000	$156,081

This hypothetical example is for illustrative purposes only, and should not be deemed a representation of past or future results, and is no guarantee of return or future performance. This example does not represent any specific product and/or service. ¹Source: Forecastchart.com - The Dow Jones Industrial Average is an index of 30 large, publicly traded companies based in the United States. Investors cannot invest directly in an index. Dividends are not included.

How did Steve end up with almost 10 times what Bill ended up with after 10 years?

The answer lies in the combination of sequence of returns coupled with reverse dollar-cost averaging. Sorry, I know that's a mouthful. I'll try to explain what that means. Anyone who has contributed to a market-based account has benefitted from dollar-cost averaging. We did it while we were working and saving. We set aside an automatic contribution from our paycheck to go into our 401(k) or 403(b), etc. and it didn't matter if the stock market was up or down, we still contributed. When the market was down, we still put money in, so we could buy more shares at their lower prices, and then they would grow more when the stock market grew back to its original position. The same, however, was true if the market was up a bit when you bought in. That portion of your investment wouldn't receive as much gain as the amounts that were purchased at lower prices, but with both of those things happening throughout your working career, it all averages in.

That tends to work pretty well when you are working and don't need to withdraw the money to live off of, but with reverse dollar-cost averaging, the opposite happens once you retire. Now you are pulling money out, so if the market goes down AND you pull money out, that increases the percent you need to get back to even, and makes it difficult for a portfolio to maintain principal. Even if the market is up a bit, when you withdraw any amount, there is less in the account to grow when the market goes up.

Steve retired in a good stock market environment. Bill, on the other hand, did not. We see Bill had three straight years of a down market, skipped a few years of positive returns, and then he ended up with a 38 percent loss in year nine! And not only was he experiencing these losses, but he was also withdrawing money from the account at the same time. So his actual dollar amount loss from the portfolio amount is that much more! As we learn from the following chart that illustrates the math of gains and losses, it takes a larger percentage gain to offset a smaller percentage loss. It's a double whammy, and as we see in Bill's example, can have a detrimental effect on a portfolio!

Unfortunately, none of us has a crystal ball and can tell what type of stock market environment we are going to retire in. There is literally a lottery effect to what the market will be like when we retire. We all know what our odds are of winning the lottery. You don't want to leave your entire retirement up to those kinds of odds.

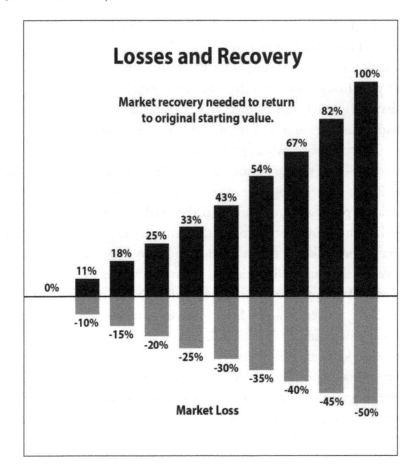

This hypothetical example is for illustrative purposes only, and should not be deemed a representation of past or future results, and is no guarantee of return or future performance. This example does not represent any specific product and/or service. The purpose of this graphic is to illustrate the percentage gains you need to offset the effect of a percentage loss on your portfolio. For example, if you started with $100,000 and lost 20 percent, as shown in column 3, your new starting value would be $80,000. To return to $100,000, you would need a gain of 25 percent to earn back your $20,000, which was 20 percent of your original amount. Similarly, if you started with $100,000 and lost 50 percent, as shown in the last column, you would need a 100 percent gain to grow from your new starting value of $50,000 to your original $100,000.

An important takeaway from this example is that it may not be the best strategy to rely on income from an account that could go down with market losses. If you do, you are subjecting yourself to the risk of reverse dollar-cost averaging. From my perspective, your core income stream in retirement should come from accounts that do not have stock market risk, in order to avoid reverse dollar-cost averaging. Always remember that investing involves risk, including the potential loss of principal. No investment strategy can guarantee a profit or protect against loss in periods of declining values.

CHAPTER 8

Your 3 Financial Phases of Life

My son, Tennyson, currently has three piggy banks. The smallest one is a white piggy bank that has little Jayhawks all over it. We live in Lawrence, Kansas, and my wife and I both attended The University of Kansas. We have to represent! The next largest piggy bank is a Jayhawk that is actually shaped like a pig. I will admit that one is a little weird looking. The largest piggy bank is a Ninja Turtle piggy bank that looks like a manhole cover and a brick wall. His grandpa is slowly helping him fill each one of them up as he brings over quarters and nickels every time he visits. There will come a time, however, when he will outgrow the piggy banks, open an actual bank account, get a job and open a retirement account, and the piggy bank phase of his life will long be over.

We all have different financial phases of our life. In all of my advising, I have come to find there are really three main phases to our financial life: the Accumulation phase, the Decumulation phase and the Distribution phase. If you are one who likes to use acronyms, I call this the ADD of retirement planning.

The Accumulation phase is the phase when we are working. This is when we will be contributing to retirement accounts on a regular basis, and the main purpose of this phase is to grow the money. In this phase we are generally younger and can take on more risk because time is on our side, and if the market does take a dive, we generally still have time to recover from those losses. Remember the explanation of dollar-cost averaging? A down market during the accumulation phase gives you the opportunity to use the same amount of money to buy more shares, since the shares are at a lower price. What I have found is that the majority of financial advisors fall into this category. They are "accumulation specialists."

The second phase, the Decumulation phase, is the phase of our life when we are either in retirement or very close to it, and now we are planning to live off of the nest egg that we spent all of our working years to create. In this phase, our money has many goals. It still needs to grow, but a good portion of it also needs to be protected because now we don't necessarily have time to wait out a downturn in the market. We are older and no longer putting money in; we are taking it out and could be victim to reverse dollar-cost averaging. Our retirement assets must also provide income that keeps up with inflation, all in the most tax-advantageous manner so as not to pay taxes unnecessarily. Our income must also last the entire life of both spouses, if married, and, when we pass, our money enters the Distribution phase, which is the phase when it passes on to our beneficiaries. The goal would be for this to be done in the most tax advantageous way possible as well in order to prevent our beneficiaries from paying taxes unnecessarily. The amount of tax is usually determined by how the assets are positioned during the Decumulation phase. The Decumulation and Distribution phases need to work well together. After considering all of the different things our money has to accomplish, can you see how there is a different skill set needed in these two phases than there is in the first phase? These last two phases are where Miller Retirement Group focuses.

Unfortunately, what I see far too often is advisors who specialize in the Accumulation phase trying to still serve their clients in the Decumulation and Distribution phases; they simply have not been trained for it, nor do they have access to financial vehicles like fixed annuities and life insurance, which are specifically designed for use in these two phases. This is an area where I would definitely like to see financial advisors start to work more like doctors. Everyone knows there are different doctors who specialize in different areas. You will never see a heart surgeon trying to perform brain surgery or your family practitioner attempting heart surgery. He or she knows that is not their area of expertise, and they know if they try to play in that area they will do more harm than good. I would like to see advisors take on more of this mindset in that aspect.

CHAPTER 9

The Financial Spectrum

I worked my way through college a number of different ways, one of them being waiting tables. What I've learned about restaurants is that they really only have three things to compete on: price, quality and service. What I have also found is that no matter the restaurant, you usually only get two out of the three! If they have great food quality and great service, don't count on a low price! You will be paying for that quality and service. And if you have a great price and great service, you're going to be sacrificing a little bit of quality. Think of McDonald's. I know people don't normally think of service when it comes to McDonald's, but if you think about it, you get your food fast every time, you know exactly what to expect, and it's cheap. Quality is questionable, though.

This experience taught me there are numerous trade-offs in life. In the financial world, there are also trade-offs. And, just like in the restaurant industry, there are three things to consider in the financial world. Those three things are **safety**, **liquidity** and **growth potential**. Just like in the restaurant industry, pick any two. I would also like to ask a question here. When you sit down with different financial advisors, what do they normally talk about? What are they trying to compete on? If I were a betting man, I would say it's growth, but I'm not betting here. They may show you past returns of all the different portfolios or mutual funds that they offer. They may talk about how their returns are better than "the other guy's" returns, but when you sit down with "that other guy" he's telling you the same thing about the first guy! And guess what, it's a statistical impossibility for both of them to be right all the time. One guy is going to beat the other guy one year and vice versa the next. A much more important question you need to ask yourself is, are your assets even in the right financial products based on the financial phase of life that you're in?

Enter the financial spectrum. At the far left-hand side of the spectrum, we are going to call this the world of principal protection and liquidity, because those are two of three aspects that you get here.

The Financial Spectrum

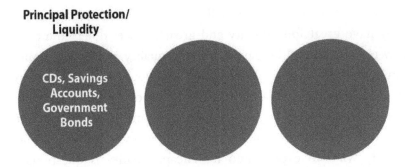

Principal Protection/
Liquidity

CDs, Savings Accounts, Government Bonds

Here you have things like checking accounts, savings accounts, certificates of deposit (CDs), money market accounts. The government also has Treasury bonds, and insurance companies have fixed annuities. Everything here is known. Your interest rate is known, you know you can't lose money due to market volatility. And, if it's something like a CD, the time period is also known. There are no surprises here. Like I mentioned earlier, the two things this world has are principal protection and liquidity. The one thing it doesn't have is growth potential. We call this world the Michael Jackson world. What dance move was Michael Jackson known for? That's right, the moonwalk. These are moonwalk accounts. These investments look like they are going forward, but once you factor in inflation vs. low interest rates, they're actually going backward. This world does a good job of safely losing purchasing power.

Next let's move all the way over to the right of the financial spectrum.

The Financial Spectrum

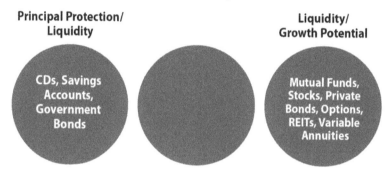

one thing it doesn't have is growth potential.

This is the world of growth and liquidity. This is where Wall Street plays. Here you will find things like stocks, bonds, mutual funds, exchange-traded funds, variable annuities and real estate investment trusts. In this category, we have **growth potential** and **liquidity**. There is even more liquidity now because of technology. You can buy and sell a stock as fast as you can click a mouse! It's highly liquid. The one thing we won't have, though, is safety. In any given year, you could experience significant gains or significant losses in the value of your investments. Those of you who remember 2008 know exactly what I mean. However, there are definitely ways to reduce the overall amount of risk you might take within this category, which I will go deeper into later.

Now we move into the middle of the financial spectrum.

The Financial Spectrum

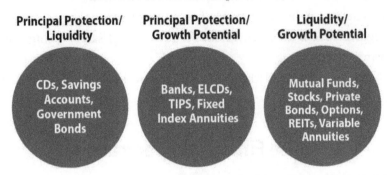

Principal Protection/ Liquidity	Principal Protection/ Growth Potential	Liquidity/ Growth Potential
CDs, Savings Accounts, Government Bonds	Banks, ELCDs, TIPS, Fixed Index Annuities	Mutual Funds, Stocks, Private Bonds, Options, REITs, Variable Annuities

The Financial Spectrum is an illustration only; it should not be construed as advice designed to meet the particular needs of an individual's situation. Please remember that any reference to principal protection or protection benefits is never a reference to securities or investment products. Bank accounts and certificates of deposit are insured by the Federal Deposit Insurance Corporation up to certain limits, government bonds are backed the U.S. Treasury Department, and annuities are backed by the financial strength and claims-paying ability of the issuing insurance company. Product features, limitations and availability may vary from state to state.

Somewhere in the middle of the spectrum is another group of financial products. They're still considered conservative because they offer principal protection — however, these products also provide the *opportunity* for greater interest or account value increases. Here we have some of the same entities we discussed at the left side of the spectrum — banks, U.S. government and insurance companies. With the banks, you will find things like equity-linked CDs. Insurance companies have fixed index annuities, and the government has things like Treasury inflation-protected securities (TIPS) and Series I savings bonds (I-bonds).

To explain the concept behind these "linked" middle bucket accounts, I'll give you the example of equity linked CDs. Back in the

90s when the stock market was basically going straight up, nobody wanted to buy a low-paying CD, but banks still issued them, so they came up with the idea of linking the interest that gets credited to the CD to some stock market index. Their principal is still protected, meaning they can't lose money as a result of market declines, but now they have more growth potential than just the run-of-the-mill, plain-vanilla CDs.

Fixed index annuities work much the same way, and have the added benefit of being tax-deferred. So, while the two features identified with this portion of the financial spectrum are **principal protection** and **growth potential**, the one thing it doesn't quite have is **liquidity**. However, let me ask you this question; do you think it is a good idea to spend 10 percent of your assets per year? If you answered no, like everyone else that I have ever asked that question to, you may be surprised to learn that many of the products in this category may provide limited liquidity. For example, most of the fixed index annuities that are available allow the owner to withdraw 10 percent per year, free of penalty, if they need to. Also, if something major were to happen, such as nursing home confinement or a terminal illness diagnosis, they may offer the benefit of being mostly or completely liquid in those instances, subject to qualification. So, in my opinion, they actually become liquid during the times when we may need them to be liquid.

So, while the two things they have are principal protection and growth potential, and the one thing they give up is liquidity, I feel like they still offer liquidity when it counts. Of course, withdrawals will reduce the contract value, as well as the value of any protection benefits. And, if you withdraw more than the "free" amount allowed each year during the contract's surrender charge period, you could end up paying a contractual fee. And, if you withdraw money before age 59 ½, it may be subject to a 10 percent additional federal tax.

The important thing about this chapter is now that we know where different types of products fall on the financial spectrum and the primary features and limitations of those products, and we also know the different phases of our financial life, we can go about figuring out where to allocate our money before we even think about returns. Knowing the characteristics of each world and knowing what you are looking for your investments to accomplish as you get closer to retirement, you and the financial advisor you work with — who specializes in the Decumulation and Distribution phases, right? — can now go about more intelligently crafting your retirement portfolio, which we will dive into deeply in a later chapter.

CHAPTER 10

Income the Wall Street Way, the Bank's Way or the Insurance Company's Way?

In order to help you more intelligently determine the income portion of your portfolio, it's important to know what vehicles are out there in order to generate income. We are told our entire lives to work hard, save diligently, invest in our 401(k), 403(b), IRA or whatever, because we are going to need that money to live off of in retirement. But then you come to retirement, and I've seen so many retirees who now have no idea how they are going to generate an income stream from these assets. They are told to save and invest their assets in order to use them for income, but they are never told how to actually go about using them for income! To me, that seems like a disconnect.

Let's look at three entities you can choose from in order to generate income in retirement. We will call these Wall Street's way, the bank's way and the insurance company's way. Let's assume that a couple needs to generate $40,000 of supplemental retirement income from their assets. How will they do it using each of these three entities?

Let's start with the bank's way. The days are gone of high-interest-earning CDs. CDs are paying such low rates now that I've had a client say that they are paying "point nothing." At the time of this writing, one-year CDs on the low side are paying .75 percent and on the high side are paying 1.25 percent. Two-year CDs are paying 1-1.52 percent. And a five-year jumbo CD, with $100,000 or more invested, is paying 1.1-2.25 percent.

CD Rates	Low	High
1-Year	0.75%	1.25%
2-Year	1.00%	1.52%
5-Year Jumbo $100,000+	1.10%	2.25%

Source: bankrate.com, Nov 2015

Let's use the five-year jumbo CD for this example. For the couple to generate $40,000 from the interest earned on the CD, they will need $1,777,777.78 in that CD! They now have no extra money for emergencies, what ifs, discretionary spending or vacations. It's all going toward that $40,000 of income, and is most likely not even keeping up with inflation.

To be fair, they are only taking out the interest as income, so you still have the $1.77 million. They still have access to it, and upon death, the $1.77 million will pass on to their beneficiaries. But they are sacrificing a lot of growth potential for a comparatively low return.

So, if we need a little bit more growth, let's now look at Wall Street's way. You must understand, though, that this is not a safe or guaranteed withdrawal rate because the value of your investments can go down with market losses. It offers the greatest potential for growth, however, so that is definitely a benefit to consider. Someone using this choice for an income stream has to understand their income could fluctuate.

This category can include dividends or interest in addition to the pure growth, but even those are not guaranteed. A common accepted income withdrawal rate used to be 4 percent of your assets. However, that was back when the stock market was going up, and we weren't seeing near the volatility we see today. There are several articles that you can Google now that will tell you the 4 percent withdrawal rate has moved down to 2.8 percent. Using the modern 2.8 percent rate of return, our hypothetical couple would need $1,428,571.43 to generate $40,000 of supplemental income. If they averaged at least 2.8 percent and only took out that 2.8 percent, our couple will also still have the full amount of their initial investment left when they pass and it will go to their beneficiaries. However, if this is the only place that they have the assets that they will use as income, what is their plan during the years when the market goes down?

Now we move on to the insurance company's way. Insurance companies use annuities of different types to generate income. Of these three different ways to generate income, insurance companies are also the only ones that can guarantee this income stream for your entire life — or you and your spouse's entire lives, if you choose to set it up that way. Insurance products like annuities are backed by the financial strength and claims-paying ability of the issuing insurance company.

I think that's important to repeat. They are not one of many choices that can guarantee this income stream for your entire life, they are the *only* place that can guarantee your income for your entire life. Your CDs can't, and neither can stocks.

By pooling risk, much the same way that life insurance works, they are generally able to offer a higher percentage payout on your money, as well. For example, a 65-year-old may be getting a 4.5 or 5 percent payout on their money, depending if he or she chose a single or joint payout.

Depending on the type of annuity you select, although there are other strings attached to get these higher payouts, you could be getting a 5.5 or 6 percent payout. And remember, this amount will be paid out for your entire life!

Let's use the smallest percentage up there, 4.5 percent, in order to see what we would need to generate that same $40,000. $888,888.89. Basically, 38 percent less than Wall Street's way, and 50 percent less than the bank's way! If we are being fair, though, I used the highest percentage rates for the other two. So, using the 6 percent example here, that would be only $666,666.67 needed.

Something to think about, though, is that if the internal growth of the annuity does not keep up with the amount you are withdrawing, it will decrease the contract's value and the value of any protection benefits. If depleted completely, the issuing company is still contractually obligated to pay the income until you or both you and your spouse pass, but at that time, there may not be any death benefit left for your beneficiaries. The death benefit in this example would come from the funds left over, if any, that did not get distributed to you as income.

You can probably see why the insurance company's way to help take care of the income needs in retirement can be an effective strategy if we find that it fits your needs. However, each "way" of generating income has its own merits. Being a fiduciary, we still have the responsibility to do what is in your best interests first, so for some this really makes sense, and for others, it may not.

As a fiduciary, I am product neutral; I am only concerned with what works best for your individual situation. In the next chapter, we will talk about how to design a portfolio. The income portion is a very important piece of your retirement portfolio's foundation, but it is not the only piece. And because it is not the only piece, we want to try to find the vehicles that will accomplish what you need using the smallest portion possible of your assets.

CHAPTER 11

Purpose-Driven Retirement Portfolio Allocation

Financial advisors first began using a version of the purpose-driven allocation model after realizing that retirees and pre-retirees have a certain thought process when it comes to long-term planning for their finances. I mentioned earlier that in the Decumulation and Distribution phases of your financial life, your money has to accomplish many things. What I realized is that the average investor thinks all of their money has to do all of those things at the same time. They think, "My money has to be safer." "I don't want to lose what I've worked 40 years to accumulate." "My money needs to provide income." "My money needs to grow to keep up with inflation. And it needs to last my entire life." Looking at a lump sum of your saved assets, that can be a little overwhelming to try to figure out.

Instead of thinking that all your money needs to perform all these different tasks at once, how about we think about it a little differently. How about we take the whole, and figure out how much is needed to perform each function, and split the total into different "buckets," each with its own function to perform. This way, each bucket only needs to accomplish one or two main functions, instead of 10 or 20, which no single investment can really do, anyway. By doing it this way, when you add the parts back into the whole, you can conceivably address all of your financial needs.

The reason I outlined the three phases of your financial life and the financial spectrum is so that once you know what the purpose of your money is, you can decide what type of financial vehicle to put it in based off of the result that financial vehicle is supposed to provide. For example, if CDs are crediting such low interest, why do people put so much money in CDs? That's right; they are most likely looking for more safety. There's really no right or wrong financial vehicle, no good or bad financial vehicle. The reason people often feel dissatisfied with a particular product is that it is the wrong vehicle for the result that the consumer is looking for.

For example, if you were looking for principal protection, and your advisor recommends putting you in stocks or a variable annuity, based off what we went through in the financial spectrum, you know that is not an appropriate recommendation. My belief is simply this: The purpose of your money directs where your money goes. If you've entered a new financial phase of your life, and you find that where you currently have your money is not where it needs to be to solve a new purpose, you should reposition your money into something that **does** get your desired result. Simple.

Now, walk with me as we create a purpose-driven portfolio together. This is going to be kept pretty high-level, without going into specific individual holdings, but I promise you will be much more informed when I am done. We will start with the foundation for a good financial strategy, and then move on from there.

We'll use a total nest egg amount of $1 million for easy math. This is, of course, a hypothetical example just to explain how a variety of financial products can be used together to provide a combination of retirement income and cash accumulation. Your actual personal situation won't necessarily look like this, which is why you should talk to a financial professional about retirement strategies, but this example can hopefully act as a springboard for that conversation.

First, let's look at what we call your liquid assets. Depending on which financial guru's book you read, it is recommended to have three to six months, or six to 12 months of living expenses in a savings account.

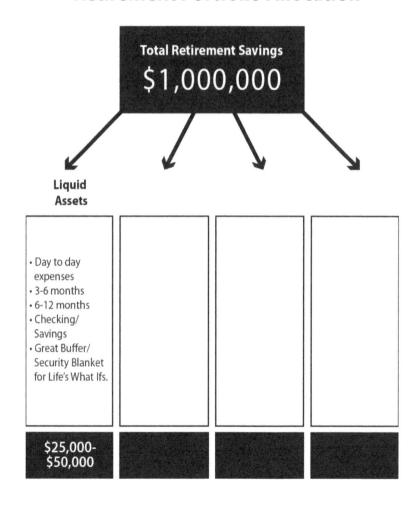

Retirement Portfolio Allocation

Total Retirement Savings
$1,000,000

Liquid Assets

• Day to day expenses
• 3-6 months
• 6-12 months
• Checking/ Savings
• Great Buffer/ Security Blanket for Life's What Ifs.

$25,000-$50,000

In retirement, with the chance of a large expenditure like long-term care being more prevalent, I like the six-to-12-month recommendation. This is where having a good handle on your budget comes into play. Your liquid assets are generally held at a bank. They will be your checking accounts, savings accounts, etc. The purpose of this bucket it is to pay your living expenses, guard against any small emergencies, and work as a general "what if" category. It can be a great security blanket; a little "buffer" for when life happens.

Next we move onto the IPA bucket. No, this is not coincidently my favorite craft beer. IPA stands for income-producing assets, and can honestly be anything that produces income. In this bucket you might see things like your pension, Social Security, (technically, Social Security is not an asset, but it is income, so it goes in this category), annuities, CDs, etc. As you have already probably figured out, the main purpose of this bucket is to produce income. This is going to be the next step in the foundation of your retirement portfolio because, no matter how you slice it, there is NO retirement without income.

This bucket creates the income that gets deposited into those liquid accounts in order to pay your basic living expenses. When it comes to your basic living expenses, would you like to see that kind of income fluctuate with the market, or would you like to see it be more stable and reliable? In other words, if the market takes a 30 percent dip, do you want your income to get cut by 30 percent, too? Personally, and I also find this is the opinion of many of my clients, I would rather see that income as stable rather than fluctuating, unless we are talking about it fluctuating only one direction, up. At bare minimum, I like to see the smallest amount necessary to at least cover our basic living expenses in this category.

Retirement Portfolio Allocation

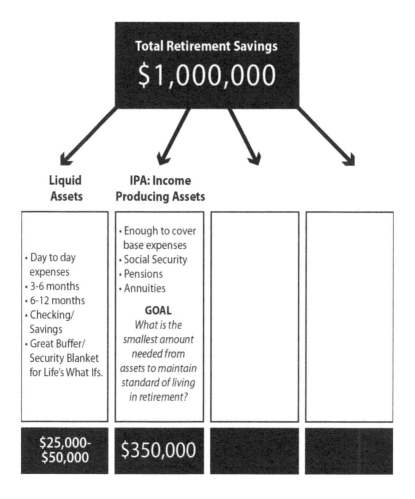

The great thing about that is you can always increase your income from that point based off of how comfortable of a retirement income stream that you want. For this example, we are simply using $350,000 of the $1 million in order to accomplish that. This leaves another $600,000 to put to work accomplishing other purposes.

The next bucket is the conservative growth bucket.

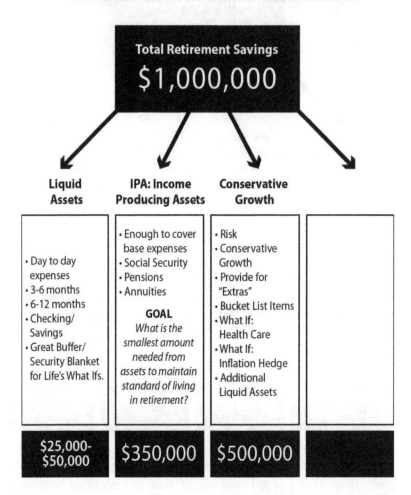

This is the portion of the portfolio where we take more risk. This bucket would include products from the right side of the financial spectrum. We prefer more conservative investments from among those products on the right side of the spectrum and will talk about how you can control the overall amount of risk in your portfolio in a later chapter. The purpose of this bucket is to grow in order to provide an inflation hedge, and possibly even generate a little bit of income while it's growing. This is also the bucket from which you should pull any money to do fun things, like travel and take vacations. All the extras! I like to say that you can call this bucket your "Bucket List" bucket. Some people may be afraid to take money out for those vacations or extras because they don't know if they'll have enough to continue living off of. This model can help give them that confidence. This bucket also provides a good next level of "what if" protection over and above the first bucket. In this example, we have put $500,000 in this bucket, leaving an even $100,000 for the next bucket.

The final bucket, if applicable, is the recovery bucket. For our clients, this usually means life insurance.

I heard someone say that in a perfect world, you spend your last dime of the first three buckets on the day you pass away, and then life insurance pays a death benefit to your beneficiaries, tax-free! Actually, in a perfect world, you've maintained your principal while taking income throughout retirement, and the life insurance helps cover any taxes that may have to be paid by your heirs on the receipt of those assets. A common misnomer about life insurance is that you have to continue paying on it for your entire life, and that's not necessarily true.

There are things called single premium paid up life insurance policies, where you pay one amount, you never have to pay again, and the policy is "paid up." The amount that this hypothetical $100,000 will purchase is based off of a lot of factors, the main ones being your age and health. Let's just assume that this $100,000 bought somewhere between $500,000 and $600,000.

You may be thinking, "Hey, that's not quite the $1 million that I started with," but how much of your IRA, which is taxable, would your beneficiaries actually be receiving after taxes? You get the idea. Once again, this hypothetical example is for illustrative purposes only, and should not be deemed a representation of past or future results, and is no guarantee of return for future performance. Further, it is not intended to provide any tax or legal advice or provide the basis for any financial decisions. You should always consult a qualified professional before making decisions about your financial situation.

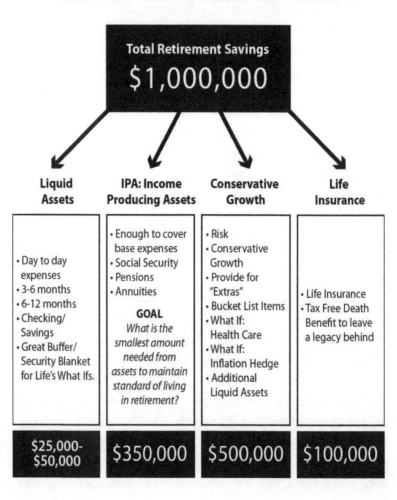

Retirement Portfolio Allocation

Total Retirement Savings
$1,000,000

Liquid Assets	IPA: Income Producing Assets	Conservative Growth	Life Insurance
• Day to day expenses • 3-6 months • 6-12 months • Checking/ Savings • Great Buffer/ Security Blanket for Life's What Ifs.	• Enough to cover base expenses • Social Security • Pensions • Annuities **GOAL** *What is the smallest amount needed from assets to maintain standard of living in retirement?*	• Risk • Conservative Growth • Provide for "Extras" • Bucket List Items • What If: Health Care • What If: Inflation Hedge • Additional Liquid Assets	• Life Insurance • Tax Free Death Benefit to leave a legacy behind
$25,000-$50,000	$350,000	$500,000	$100,000

The underlying current of all four of these buckets should be a current of tax efficiency so that both you and your beneficiaries pay the least amount of tax possible. We outlined a little of this earlier.

CHAPTER 12

How Much Risk
C.A.N. You Handle?

O bviously, based on the title of this chapter, this is an acro-
nym. As we dive deeper into risk, how many of you have
sat down with a financial professional and filled out a
risk-profile questionnaire? This is a questionnaire that customarily
places you into one of three risk categories as an investor: conservative, moderate or aggressive. As a matter fact, you've probably been asked to describe yourself as one of those three types of
investors based on the level of risk you are willing to assume.

I believe this is one of the worst questions out there, and that
hundreds of thousands, and millions of dollars are invested based
upon what I believe to be faulty assumptions. If I had 20 retirees in
a room — and I have, so this isn't actually as random as I'm making
it out to be — and I asked what one person's definition of conservative was, it won't be the same as the next person's. As a matter of fact, spouses often have different definitions!

The problem with this risk profile questionnaire is that once
you fill it out and you fit into whatever category as they have de-
fined it, that is where you live from then on. Allow me to give an
analogy of why I believe this is a bad practice. Let me ask you a

question: under normal circumstances, if you are driving down the interstate, and the speed limit is 75, how fast are you going? If you are like me, you have probably set the cruise over 80 but less than 85. Let's settle on 82. So this risk profile questionnaire sets the speed of your portfolio at 82. So now we are flying, I mean driving safely, down the interstate. Now let me ask you this, if it is raining heavily, and you have your windshield wipers on high, how fast are you probably going now? For arguments' sake, let's just say we have slowed down to 40 miles an hour. The problem with this risk profile questionnaire is that no matter what the road conditions are, they still have you going 82 miles an hour! It could be 2008, and your portfolio is still going 82. You can see how this could be a problem. We are going to call this your capacity for risk.

Capacity

A

N

So, if your capacity for risk is set at 82 miles an hour, the problem is that it is not always sunny and 75 degrees in the markets. Storms come (2008), and when they hit, they can hit hard.

So the next thing that we need to establish is an individualized definition of risk. This is going to be your attitude toward risk.

Capacity

Attitude

N

I want to tell you the story of a couple, we will call them Mr. and Mrs. Smith. They had $1.2 million saved up in retirement assets. When asking Mrs. Smith, "How much money do you feel you could afford to lose in any one year before you would be really concerned?"

She told me "Honestly, if I lose anything with six figures, I am going to have some serious concerns." Her husband however, was able to stomach a little more risk. He said, "I could probably stand to see about $150,000 to $200,000 before I would really be concerned about taking money out of these accounts to live off of." To round that off, we will just call it 15 percent, maximum. The most they were willing to risk in any year was 15 percent of their portfolio. This was their attitude toward risk.

Finally, we needed to establish how much need they had for risk.

Capacity

Attitude

Need

In order to do this, we needed to find out how much income they needed to pull from their portfolio every year in order to supplement Social Security, any pensions they may have or any other income streams. In this case, they needed an additional $48,000 a year, or 4 percent, from their retirement assets to support their lifestyle. We would like to see an extra 2 to 3 percent in order to keep up with inflation.

So it looks like this:

$1,200,000 retirement savings

$48,000 income needed

4 percent of portfolio

2-3 percent more needed for inflation

They need to average a 6 – 7 percent rate of return to support their income needs and account for inflation.

We need to talk now about something called *total return*. Total return equals yield plus gain. Yield would be the interest if we are talking about a CD or a bond, and the dividends if we are talking about stock. Gain is what we normally think of when we look at the price of a stock, and we see that it gained 5 percent for the year. Those two numbers added together equal your total return. Yield + gain= total return.

You can also think of it like this: If you have a rental house, your rent is your cash flow, or yield. If your property appreciates in value, that is considered your gain. The gain, just like in the market, is never actually realized until it is sold. Rent - expenses = cash flow. Interest or dividends - fees = cash flow.

Hopefully that wasn't too confusing, but the reason we use this is to find out whether or not a portfolio is set up in line with a client's capacity, attitude and need. In this example, when we ran our stress test and fee analysis on Mr. and Mrs. Smith's portfolio, we found it said that going forward, this portfolio should average 7.58 percent. Not bad, right?

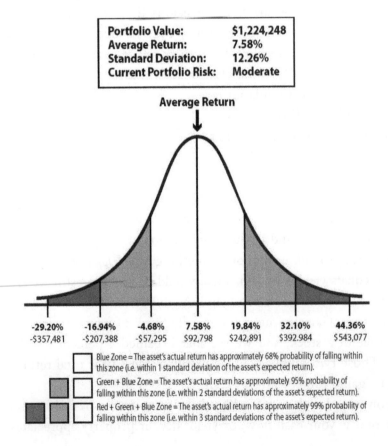

That fell in line with the 6 to 7 percent needed, so that's OK. However, if we look at this bell curve, we see that, while their portfolio may have had a possibility of a 44 percent gain in any one year, it also had the potential for a 30 percent loss. So, going back to the normal risk profile questionnaire, the financial company was basically saying they should be willing to lose 29 percent in any one year. Well, we knew that was out of line with their attitude, so right away we recognized their portfolio was off. Now, you may be saying "Yes, but that is simply an algorithm that your software ran on how they think it will perform based off their current holdings. How do we know whether or not it is accurate?" Well, let's look at this next bit.

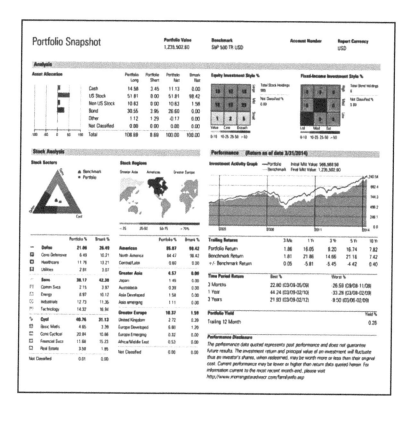

The couple's portfolio snapshot may look confusing, but if you look at the right hand column, toward the bottom with the heading, "Time Period Returns," we saw the worst single year loss was 33.28 percent! That's right in line with the bell curve, and based off their 15 percent maximum attitude toward risk, it was definitely NOT OK! The question we needed to ask was: "Would you be willing to lose 33 percent in order to average 7 percent?

Speaking of attitude toward risk, let's look at the chart just above the Time Period Returns that has the highlighted area and the solid line. The highlighted area is the performance of the S&P 500 index. The solid line is the performance of their current portfolio. Do you see how they move together? This means they were still highly correlated with the market. By correlated with the market, I mean the value of their assets moved up and down basically at the same time as the stock market, so this shows the Smiths were still invested with the same amount of risk as they were in 2008.

Do you think they probably sat down with their advisor after 2008 and made some changes? Whatever those changes were, they were still exposed to the same amount of risk years later. That was obviously incorrect, based on their personal definition of risk, which should have mattered more than some arbitrary company's definition.

Let's leave that behind for a second, now, and move on to the yield. Mr. and Mrs. Smith said that they needed — $48,000, or 4 percent, per year. That would be their yield. Looking at this report, we saw their yield was 0.26 percent. This was also not fine, and was not in line with their goals. That was exacerbated even further when we found out what their fees were. Their fees were 1.93 percent per year! That's like saying, we'll pay you $3,183.04 per year as long as we can pay ourselves $23,627.98 per year! Seems fair, right? WRONG!

A very important thing to consider is this: Once it is time to take income in retirement, a fundamental shift in our life is taking place. We also need to have a fundamental shift in how we think about our investments.

The marketing machine known as Wall Street would have you believe that the growth or gain of the investment is the ultimate gauge of whether or not it is successful. Now that we are retiring and we are getting ready to draw income off of our retirement assets, we need to shift that mindset to look for **cash flow percentages** that can affect our lifestyles in retirement rather than **gain percentages**. We should focus on asking "What percentage of cash flow can I get on my money?" not "What percentage gain can I get on my money?"

Here's why I didn't like the Smiths' original portfolio. It relied solely on the market in order to be successful.

I want to show what I call "The Tale of Two Portfolios." We are going to look at two separate portfolios that have almost identical average returns and each have the same amount of withdrawals, and once again show you how average return does not matter as much as not only the sequence of returns, but also the volatility of the market.

Whether you believe the market is going to trend up or down or even sideways for the next 10 years is irrelevant, but I think we can all agree that, no matter what direction that it trends, it may be an extremely volatile ride to that end.

The first set of charts illustrates the returns of the S&P 500 from 2000 to 2015, and then those same returns reversed, each taking the same $50,000 each year.

Year	S&P 500	S&P 500			
		Beg Bal	Earnings	Withdrawal	End Bal
2000	-9.10%	$1,000,000	-$91,000	-$50,000	$859,000
2001	-11.89%	$859,000	-$102,135	-$50,000	$706,865
2002	-22.10%	$706,865	-$156,217	-$50,000	$500,648
2003	28.68%	$500,648	$10,586	-$50,000	$594,234
2004	10.88%	$594,234	$64,653	-$50,000	$608,886
2005	4.91%	$608,886	$29,896	-$50,000	$588,782
2006	15.79%	$588,782	$92,969	-$50,000	$631,751
2007	5.49%	$631,751	$34,683	-$50,000	$616,434
2008	-37.00%	$616,434	-$228,081	-$50,000	$338,354
2009	26.46%	$338,354	$89,528	-$50,000	$377,882
2010	15.06%	$377,882	$56,909	-$50,000	$384,791
2011	2.11%	$384,791	$8.119	-$50,000	$342,910
2012	16.00%	$342,910	$54,866	-$50,000	$347,776
2013	32.39%	$347,776	$112,645	-$50,000	$410,420
2014	13.69%	$410,420	$56,187	-$50,000	$416,607
2015	-0.73%	$416,607	-$3,027	-$50,000	$363,580
average	5.67%	Total Distributions: -$800,000			
std dev	18.69%				

These tables are intended to illustrate the potential results of a hypothetical investment of $1,000,000 in the S&P 500 Index beginning on the first trading day of 2000 and held through the last trading day of 2015. It is assumed that any dividends and other earnings are reinvested and no allowances for external advisory fees have been made. The results may vary significantly if the beginning day/and or the ending day is altered. Please note, it is not possible to invest directly in the S&P 500. This measure is simply provided as a general gauge of overall market performance. The Index performance and other information was acquired from Yahoo! Finance. It is believed to be accurate but has not been independently verified. Past performance is not necessarily indicative of future results.

Year	S&P 500 Reversed	S&P 500 Reversed			
		Beg Bal	Earnings	Withdrawal	End Bal
2000	-0.73%	$1,000,000	-$7,266	-$50,000	$942,734
2001	13.69%	$942,734	$129,060	-$50,000	$1,021,794
2002	32.39%	$1,021.794	$330,959	-$50,000	$1,302,753
2003	16.00%	$1,302,753	$208,441	-$50,000	$1,461,194
2004	2.11%	$1,461,194	$30,831	-$50,000	$1,442,025
2005	15.06%	$1,442,025	$217,169	-$50,000	$1,609,194
2006	26.46%	$1,609,194	$425,793	-$50,000	$1,984,987
2007	-37.00%	$1,984,987	-$734,445	-$50,000	$1,200,542
2008	5.49%	$1,200,542	$65,910	-$50,000	$1,216,452
2009	15.79%	$1,216,452	$192,078	-$50,000	$1,358,529
2010	4.91%	$1,358,529	$66,704	-$50,000	$1,375,233
2011	10.88%	$1,375,233	$149,625	-$50,000	$1,474,858
2012	28.68%	$1,474,858	$422,989	-$50,000	$1,847,848
2013	-22.10%	$1,847,848	-$408,374	-$50,000	$1,389,473
2014	-11.89%	$1,389,473	-$165,208	-$50,000	$1,174,265
2015	-9.10%	$1,174,265	-$106,858	-$50,000	$1,017,407
average	5.67%	Total Distributions: -$800,000			
std dev	18.69%				

As you'll see at the bottom, they have the exact same "average return," but the dollar amount result is over $650,000 different! And it needed some pretty big gains to offset those huge losses. (Let's also not forget — that larger number didn't actually occur, because that is the one that would have been the S&P returns in reverse.) And if you want to add "investor behavior" into the mix, I don't know how many retirees would have been comfortable continuing to pull $50,000 out after 2002, when they have 50 percent of what they started with!

The charts illustrate your portfolio may have gained some back eventually, but when you're in the middle of it, you don't have the luxury of looking at a chart that shows you'll get through it! That affects your spending confidence, and therefore, your quality of life in retirement.

The next pair of illustrations show a conservative actively managed account with a slightly lower "average return."

Year	Low Volatility Index	Low Volatility Portfolio			
		Beg Bal	Earnings	Withdrawal	End Bal
2000	8.5%	$1,000,000	$85,040	-$50,000	$1,035,040
2001	-3.05%	$1,035,040	-$31,597	-$50,000	$953,444
2002	3.31%	$953,444	$31,595	-$50,000	$935,039
2003	15.16%	$935,039	$141,772	-$50,000	$1,026,811
2004	8.42%	$1,026,811	$86,443	-$50,000	$1,063,255
2005	8.45%	$1,063,255	$89,800	-$50,000	$1,103,055
2006	5.37%	$1,103,055	$59,280	-$50,000	$1,112,335
2007	10.02%	$1,112,335	$111,414	-$50,000	$1,173,749
2008	-0.89%	$1,173,749	-$10,428	-$50,000	$1,113.321
2009	3.92%	$1,113,321	$36,656	-$50,000	$1,099,977
2010	11.76%	$1,099.977	$129,351	-$50,000	$1,179,328
2011	11.06%	$1,179,328	$130,379	-$50,000	$1,259,707
2012	5.47%	$1,259,649	$68,942	-$50,000	$1,278,649
2013	-1.95%	$1,278,649	-$24,909	-$50,000	$1,203,740
2014	9.49%	$1,203,740	$114,177	-$50,000	$1,267,917
2015	-5.47%	$1,267,917	-$69,325	-$50,000	$1,148,592
average	5.56%	Total Distributions: -$800,000			
std dev	5.92%				

These tables are intended to illustrate the potential results of a hypothetical investment of $1,000,000 in a hypothetical mix of securities, which would yield a series of returns that are less volatile than the returns of an investment intended to track the S&P 500 over the same time period, beginning on the first trading day of 2000 and held through the last trading day of 2015. The table does not represent the results of an investment in an actual security or mix of securities.

Year	Low Volatility Reversed	Low Volatility Portfolio Reversed			
		Beg Bal	Earnings	Withdrawal	End Bal
2000	-5.47%	$1,000,000	-$54,676	-$50,000	$895,324
2001	9.49%	$895,324	$84,923	-$50,000	$930,247
2002	-1.95%	$930,247	-$18,122	-$50,000	$862,125
2003	5.47%	$862,125	$47,183	-$50,000	$859,308
2004	11.06%	$859,308	$95,000	-$50,000	$904,308
2005	11.76%	$904,308	$106,341	-$50,000	$960,649
2006	3.29%	$960,649	$31,629	-$50,000	$942,278
2007	-0.89%	$942,278	-$8,372	-$50,000	$883,907
2008	10.02%	$883,907	$88,534	-$50,000	$922,441
2009	5.37%	$922,441	$49,574	-$50,000	$922,014
2010	8.45%	$922,014	$77,871	-$50,000	$949,886
2011	8.42%	$949,886	$79,967	-$50,000	$979,853
2012	15.16%	$979,853	$148,567	-$50,000	$1,078,420
2013	3.31%	$1,078,420	$35,737	-$50,000	$1,064,157
2014	-3.05%	$1,064,157	-$32,486	-$50,000	$981,671
2015	8.50%	$981,671	$83,482	-$50,000	$1,015,153
average	5.56%	Total Distributions: -$800,000			
std dev	5.92%				

Look at the ending amounts, though. They are much closer together. Within $133,000 of each other rather than off by $650,000! And quite a few of the second illustration's years have pretty meager returns, yet the "standard deviation," or the volatility, is lower. In all actuality, the performance of this portfolio is rather boring! However, it looks like boring is good! My clients love boring! The bottom line, and what I really want you to understand from these illustrations, is that in retirement you can live with low return years. What you absolutely cannot live with is BIG LOSSES! You have to be willing to give up some of the upside in order to avoid the big downside. You don't have to hit homeruns in retirement in order to be successful, but time and again, we find portfolios that are swinging for the fences! All you really have to do is hit singles and doubles, and simply avoid the big strikeouts!

These risk, fee and yield reports are what we run in the normal process of our retirement planning. We call it our Resuscitation Report. If you have not determined your capacity, attitude or need for risk, nor seen how your current portfolio is exposed to risk, you may want to find that out as soon as possible! Don't become the victim of another 2008! Don't go one more week without understanding your risk exposure!

CHAPTER 13

Fiduciary vs. Suitability

Financial services can be very complex and obscure for even sophisticated members of the investing public. You don't need to understand everything, but it is critical to understand the motivation behind the person offering you financial products or advice. Now, I will admit that the title of this chapter has a couple of funny sounding words.

Fiduciary is basically a fancy sounding word to describe someone who has gone through the necessary steps to hold themselves and their practice to the highest standard of financial advising responsibility. It means that they now have a legal liability to do what is in the best interest of their client. I want you to hear that again. It means now they have a legal responsibility to do what is in the best interest of their client. You may be asking yourself, "Don't all financial professionals have to do that anyway?" And the answer, unfortunately, is no.

Now, it is my personal belief that most financial professionals out there do operate in their client's best interest from a moral standpoint; at least I would hope so. But the truth is, from a legal standpoint, not all financial professionals are held to that higher standard.

The standard that many financial professionals are held to is what is known as a suitability standard. The suitability standard does not require a financial professional to always act in your best interest; rather, it requires them to make product recommendations that are suitable for you based on your financial needs and goals. While the suitability standard is a good standard, in my opinion, someone who is held to a suitability standard is more focused on products than clients. A broker, as they are normally referred to, operates from a suitability standard. They offer products for sale from a range of companies they represent, and are paid commissions from those companies, calculated as a percentage of the amount you invest. For example, if a broker sells a mutual fund with an upfront load of 5 percent, that 5 percent is the commission paid to the broker on that mutual fund. That commission is paid by the investor. So to use simple math, if you invested $100,000 into a mutual fund with a 5 percent upfront load, you are beginning with only $95,000 in your mutual fund.

An "advisor," the word we will use to represent someone with a fiduciary standard, offers "best advice" taking into account the needs of each client's individual situation, and are paid by a residual fee that is calculated as a percentage of the total assets under advisement. In this capacity, they only make more money if they help you make more money. So the incentive of the advisor is aligned with the client.

I do need to clarify, however, that a number of fiduciary advisors are licensed to offer insurance products like life insurance and annuities that pay a commission in addition to receiving the asset-based fee compensation. That could also offer a potential conflict of interest. I want to point out a big difference in how that commission is paid, though. With the mutual fund load, the commission is coming from the investor's assets and reduces the amount the investor actually puts in the financial vehicle. With an insurance commission, the issuing insurance company pays the commission to the advisor, and therefore the advisor's pay doesn't reduce the amount that the investor puts into the financial vehicle. Plus, the advisor is still held to a fiduciary standard, so their recommendation ultimately has to be in your best interests.

Now this doesn't mean that there are a bunch of Bernie Madoffs running around if they are not held to a fiduciary standard, it simply means that their goals may not necessarily be aligned with the client's.

So why should you care? There are two main reasons for ensuring that you're working with a fiduciary advisor, rather than a broker with a suitability standard. One of those is cost. In many circumstances these "retail" products that are sold have upfront commissions and undisclosed internal costs that can erode your returns. The second reason is motivation. Like I mentioned, brokers get paid to sell you products. Their motivation is to sell you more and more products to earn commissions, and they can actually recommend products with higher commissions than other products that may meet your needs better. Fiduciary advisors cannot. Fiduciary advisors are paid for the advice and management they give you and are not focused on a product sale.

Someone who operates under the fiduciary standard, and has your best interest in mind, will have the title of Investment Adviser Representative, and may own their own Registered Investment Adviser firm. I suggest that, especially in your retirement years, you work with someone who has their goals aligned with your own, and not someone with their own agenda.

CHAPTER 14

CPR Retirement Rescue Roadmap

In the summer of 2015, people called me a hero after failing to save someone's life.

On July 17, 2015, in Colorado, after summiting Mount Yale, my first Fourteener, I and my two hiking buddies, Charlie and Aaron, got hit by a storm on our descent before we were able to reach the shelter of the tree line. The wind was blowing so hard that the sleet and hail were coming at us sideways. All of a sudden, we saw a lightning bolt strike the mountain less than 100 yards in front of us, so we decided to take momentary shelter among some rocks until the storm let up a bit.

After a few minutes, we continued on only to come upon four people who had been hit by that lightning. They were part of two different hiking parties. Two of them were brothers. The other two, Ryan and Katie, were husband and wife. The two brothers were the farthest from the strike, so were not hurt very badly. Unfortunately, the husband-wife team wasn't as lucky. As we came upon them, one of the brothers had already started CPR on the wife, who took the direct hit. Charlie happens to be a firefighter, and Aaron is ex-military. This being his fourth or fifth Fourteener, Aaron was the fastest and most experienced hiker among us, so we sent him down the mountain to get help while Charlie and I stayed and performed CPR on Katie.

Ryan, her husband, was right there giving rescue breaths the entire time. We performed CPR on her for 45 minutes with no response before Charlie decided to call it. I will never forget what he said, because I remember how impressed I was with his delivery of the news. It was straightforward, yet still tactful and full of sensitivity. There is no way I would've been able to deliver that kind of news with that amount of composure.

His words were, "Ryan look at me. We need to talk. We've been doing CPR on Katie for over half an hour now with no response. It might be time to start thinking about the fact that she may not be coming back. We'll keep doing CPR as long as you want us to, though. It's your call." Ryan knew she was gone. He gave her two more breaths, then kissed her for the last time.

Right after that kiss, any hope of his bride coming back now gone, Ryan self-destructed and tried to kill himself by bashing his head on an adjacent boulder while screaming, "I just want to die! It should've been me!"

I tackled him off the rock and held him in a full nelson to keep him from doing any more damage to himself. We struggled to the ground, me on the bottom, on my back, still holding him on top of me in the full nelson, while the others scrambled to help subdue him. Eventually, he gave in. Our focus turned to him, to keeping him alive, when we were hit by a second storm! All of us exhausted from the CPR, shivering, crying, we weathered through the storm together before we found a small crag between some rocks up the mountain a bit to shelter us from the wind.

As a team, we carried Ryan to it, and there we hunkered down, waiting hours longer before a search-and-rescue team found us. We struggled to keep Ryan awake until our rescuers arrived. The first search-and-rescue paramedic on scene assigned me the task of mapping a route down the mountain to a clearing large enough for a helicopter to land, about a half-mile trek from our shelter. I needed to find the safest route, knowing that we had to carry Ryan the entire way and not fall and break a leg in the process.

By the time the paramedic finished assessing Ryan, and was ready to start carrying him, I found a route. I started to lead our party down, but Ryan continued to slip further and further from consciousness. It wasn't long before he was completely unresponsive and the men carrying his limp body grew tired. We switched duties, and I shouldered in to help carry. I had already mapped out the route, though, and I knew exactly where we needed to go and where we needed to step. We made it there with no one falling. Ryan made it to the helicopter, then to the hospital, and was in critical condition for the next two days, but made it.

While we weren't able to save Katie, we were able to save Ryan's life. Once I was back home, getting called a hero didn't make the experience any better. As a kid, you make believe about being a superhero, of having power, of saving people. No one ever dreams of being called a hero when you DON'T save someone.

You are probably wondering why am I telling you this story, what it could possibly have to do with retirement planning? And that's a very valid question.

The best way that I can answer: Everyone becomes the sum total of all of the experiences they have had in life, and how they choose to respond to them. And I've chosen to use my experiences on that mountain as inspiration rather than a focus of desperation. It could have easily been me who was struck by lightning. I could be all "woe is me that I had to go through something like this," or I could realize that I was given a gift. I had better get busy making the most out of this life now because it could literally be over in a flash.

I think it is important to note here that this was the second person I have performed CPR on. The first was while I was a student athletic trainer in college during a track practice one afternoon. I was able to save her life, but she was not struck by lightning. I believe there was nothing we could have done to save Katie's life. I believe she passed instantly. It's an understatement to say an experience like that is life-changing, but when I said I decided to use the experience as inspiration rather than desperation, it inspired me to name my planning process in her honor, and that is how I came up with the CPR Retirement Rescue Roadmap. I realized that every day I am resuscitating peoples' financial lives. And to be perfectly honest, there will be some retirements that I will be able to resuscitate, and some that I won't. They will simply be too far gone. Like in Katie's situation, there may be nothing that I can do, but just like in Ryan's case, my actions could help determine whether or not you will make it down the mountain with confidence.

It also inspired me to write a book that goes more into detail about that experience, that entire day, and even some stories since the experience, and I have decided to donate any and all profits from that book to different charities close to Katie's heart. Ryan's brother set up a GoFundMe page for Katie right after her passing, with proceeds going to multiple places, including a scholarship fund at her place of work — she was a teacher — and also the American Association for the Care of Children, an organization through which she had gone on mission trips to Nicaragua. She was a good person, taken from this world too soon. This is my way of carrying on her legacy of giving even after she is gone. I never knew her while she was alive, but I felt a strong calling to honor her in this way.

So, with all that being said, The CPR Retirement Rescue Roadmap goes through three steps.

1. The Triage Visit
2. The Resuscitation Report
3. The Retirement Rescue Roadmap

In the Triage Visit we will sit down and get to know each other. Together we will identify any areas of concern that you may have in regards to your retirement, what is important to you, where your investments are, and what you would like them to accomplish. Just like when you arrive on the scene to any emergency situation, you first and foremost have to recognize that it is an emergency in order to act with the necessary speed. You must gather information about the scene in order to know how to proceed. That is exactly what we will be doing in the Triage Visit; gathering information. I lay it all out on the table, like I'm doing right now with this story, and because of this I don't feel that I can make any recommendations about something as important as your money until I get to know you. I also don't want there to be any pressure at all in this first visit. As a matter fact, I do not accept clients on the first visit. No recommendations will be made during this visit. No assets will be moved. No allocations changed. We are simply getting to know each other to find out whether or not we will be a good fit for each other.

Next, during the Resuscitation Report, I will report my findings based off all of the information that I gathered during our first visit.

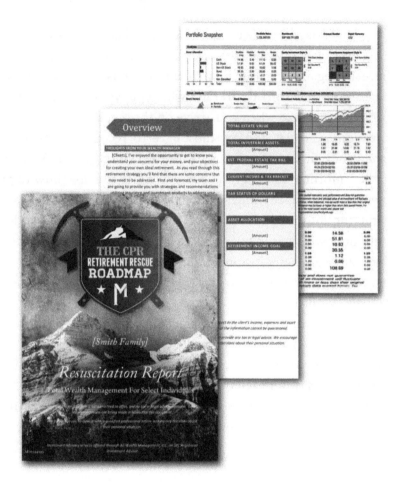

This will include analyzing your current situation from top to bottom. We will stress test your portfolio to determine your current level of exposure to market risk. We will look at your income streams in retirement and determine if they are sufficient to meet your needs. We will analyze your fees, too, so you know exactly what you are paying, and we will determine together whether or not everything is aligned with your financial goals, or if you are open to some different perspectives to potentially improve your situation. If so, we will get to work to resuscitate your retirement!

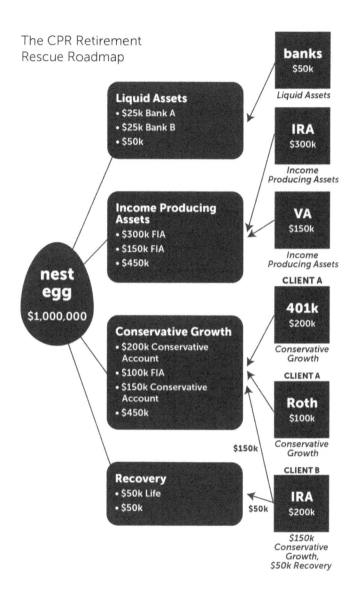

The CPR Retirement Rescue Roadmap

This hypothetical example is for illustrative purposes only. It should not be construed as advice designed to meet the particular needs of an individual's situation.

Finally, we come to the Retirement Rescue Roadmap. We will now have a co-created strategy for your retirement, taking into account everything you have read so far: Which phase of life you are in and therefore what amounts need to be where on the financial spectrum, where you will be generating your income... Everything will have an underlying current of tax efficiency. I will then take stock of all of your different holdings, and they will be completely outlined for you in one single, easy-to-read document, your Retirement Roadmap. I believe in simplicity. This won't only be in one document, I will put it on one page.

Whether that particular account is with me or not, you will have a consolidated map that points to your resources and your financial goals.

If you think of your financial life like a mountain, the Accumulation phase is the trek up the mountain. Retirement is the summit. The trek back down is the Decumulation phase. That's the phase that many don't plan adequately for, both in mountain climbing and retirement. Statistically, the majority of climbing fatalities happen on the way down a mountain. And, if something happens to your retirement on the way down, like a lightning strike, you can rest assured I'll be there to carry YOU down the mountain.

Nathaniel J. (Nate) Miller's financial advice is focused on helping baby boomers and retirees build simplified, more conservative financial strategies to give them more confidence in their financial futures.

Nate was born and raised on a farm in Morrowville, Kansas; hard, honest work has been bred into him from the beginning. He graduated from Barton County Community College, studying athletic training and theater, before attending The University of Kansas, where he studied business.

While still in college he started his five-year tax preparation career, then moved into the regulatory side of the banking industry, performing audits on community banks. This was during the financial meltdown, giving him great insight into the inner workings of what led to that.

In 2010, he joined Advisors Excel, one of the largest financial marketing organizations in the country, and consulted for financial advisors who specialize in retirement planning for baby boomers and retirees. He quickly obtained his insurance licenses and became registered as an Investment Adviser Representative and began splitting time between consulting financial advisors, and running his own financial services practice. Nate took full advantage of his exposure to some of the brightest financial minds in the U.S., learning the different financial disciplines of these elite advisors, and, picking out the best pieces, developed his own retirement planning process and low-volatility investing discipline.

With a deep sense of responsibility to help people retire the right way and a thorough understanding of a wide variety of financial products, Nate decided to leave his well-paying consulting career and dedicate his focus and time fully to helping people pursue their financial goals and prepare for more confident retirements.

Nate currently resides in Lawrence, Kansas, with his wife and child.

ACKNOWLEDGEMENTS

M y 36 years on this planet comprises many zigs and zags. Going through the complete list of people who had a huge impact on my life would take many pages, and I would inadvertently forget some. There is a handful, though, to whom I would like to draw special attention.

First would be my parents, Fred and Diane Miller, who always told me I could be or do anything I wanted. While we may not have had a lot of money growing up, we were never poor in the areas of life that truly count.

Another thank you would go out to Matt Neuman for introducing me to a different side of financial planning than I originally considered. Working alongside him to consult financial advisors across the country gave me the vision for my own practice. I had the extreme fortune to consult advisors who truly have a heart for this business, and their advising style sincerely reflected the fact that they cared deeply about their clients and their success in retirement.

I couldn't finish this without acknowledging Charlie and Aaron, my two buddies who were with me on Mt. Yale. Going through that experience has brought all of us closer together, and without the ability to lean on you afterward, I don't believe that I would've gotten through it as well as I have. Aaron, there's no way I could've made it down the mountain as fast as you did. You truly are half mountain goat. Charlie, without your first responder experience and impressive coolness under pressure, I don't know if

Ryan would've made it off that mountain alive. You were a rock in that situation, and led everyone involved. I love you both.

I also need to thank my lovely, infinitely patient and supportive wife, Melissa. When I finally decided to leave my stable, six-figure-paying job in order to follow my dreams, there was no hesitation on her part. She actually told me she wondered why I hadn't done it sooner. She has unwavering faith in me. The type of faith that a man needs to know his wife has for him. I love you, Hon.

Finally, I would like to thank God. I've had so many events in my life or directions I could've gone or choices that I could have made that, while at the time seemed inconsequential, when looking back on it all, everything was working together in ways I never could've imagined. I'd like to think that some of my success has to do with me, but there is a very large part of it that I didn't play any part in, and could only be explained by His grace.